P9-CRL-860

Additional Praise

"When you ask someone how they got a scar, you're in for an entertaining story, but you're also asking them to uncover past trauma. *The Day the Klan Came to Town*, is the story of a town's past trauma, one that left a scar that has been masterfully explored and retold by Campbell and Khodabandeh. The book is a poignant example of the shared trauma of bigotry and violence in America, while also providing a stunning example of the power that a cohesive and empathetic community could have against the forces of violence and suppression.

—Jason Rodriguez,
editor of *APB: Artists against Police Brutality*, *Voces Sin Fronteras*,
and *Colonial Comics* Vols. 1 & 2

"In the 1920s, the KKK had around four million members across the United States. Their rallies, manifestations of racism and xenophobia, were commonplace across America. In 1927, for instance, in Jamaica, Queens, several KKK members were arrested in the aftermath of such a rally, among them Queens resident Fred Trump.

In *The Day the Klan Came to Town* Bill Campbell and Bizhan Khodabandeh therefore shed light on an important piece of American history. The graphic novel, based on a rally that occurred in Campbell's hometown in 1923, is, however, not primarily about the Klan, but rather a story about immigrants, unity and hope that echoes the famous lines in Emma Lazarus poem Emma Lazarus's poem 'The New Colossus'—Give me your tired, your poor, your huddled masses yearning to breathe free.

In a time, when the son of a KKK member has recently been U.S. president, this book is an important reminder of America's true greatness: diversity."

—Julian Voloj,
author of *Ghetto Brother: Warrior
to Peacemaker* and *Basquiat*

"Bill Campbell continues to do society a service by sharing the important stories that help us to be better. Understanding American history will put us on a path to being better than our past selves. *The Day the Klan Came to Town* is an example of an uncelebrated story that shows us where we have been and helps us grow into the society we need to be."

—Joel Christian Gill,
illustrator of *Strange Fruit*

"Sound familiar? An invading hate group, a corrupt police force, and ineffectual government force a diverse cross section of town residents to fight back. Through the use of comics, intensive research, and their vivid imaginations, Campbell and Khodabandeh bring to life the infamous 'Karnegie Day' riot of August 25, 1923. Carnegie's largely Catholic townspeople resist internal resentments and infighting to band together against the Klan. Throughout the narrative we get a sense of the town's history and the immigrants who settled there — ironically many of them fleeing persecution in their home countries. This nearly century-old story is echoed in today's movements for social change."

—Josh Neufeld,
author of *A.D.: New Orleans after the Deluge*

The Day the Klan Came to Town

Written by Bill Campbell
Art by Bizhan Khodabandeh

The Day the Klan Came to Town
Written by Bill Campbell • Illustrated by Bizhan Khodabandeh
© Bill Campbell and Bizhan Khodabandeh 2021
This edition © PM Press 2021
All rights reserved. No part of this book may be transmitted by any means without permission in writing from the publisher

PM Press
PO Box 23912
Oakland, CA 94623
www.pmpress.org
ISBN (paperback): 978-1-62963-872-0
ISBN (ebook): 978-1-62963-894-2
Library of Congress Control Number: 2020947294

10 9 8 7 6 5 4 3 2 1
Printed in the USA

Foreword by P. Djèlí Clark

"Unlimited tolerance must lead to the disappearance of tolerance. If we extend unlimited tolerance even to those who are intolerant, if we are not prepared to defend a tolerant society against the onslaught of the intolerant, then the tolerant will be destroyed, and tolerance with them."

—Karl Popper, *The Open Society and Its Enemies* (1945)

"'cause now we got chromes to put them where they belong"

—Gang Starr, *Tonz 'O' Gunz* (1994)

I first met Bill Campbell back in early 2013, by way of an invitation to submit to his forthcoming anthology for, by, and about people of color, called *Mothership: Tales from Afrofuturism and Beyond*. I submitted but I didn't get in. Thems the breaks. Bill and I remained in contact. We ran into each other at cons and other genre events, where we chopped it up often about his harrowing tales of tackling the fraught issues of diversity (or lack thereof) in SFF spaces.

So when I first heard about his plans for this graphic novel, I was immediately intrigued. At the time I was working on my own story of resistance and racism, in a novella called *Ring Shout*. The story Bill tells here is set in the same era, during the rise of the Second Klan, founded in the wake of D.W. Griffith's infamous 1915 film *The Birth of a Nation*. Unlike the first Invisible Empire, this reincarnation was not confined to the states of the former Confederacy. By the 1920s, the Second Klan had mounted a vigorous mobilization campaign, spreading throughout the Midwest, the East Coast, and as far as Seattle, Washington. This Second Klan also extended its list of "undesirables." While African Americans remained victims of their terrorism, the enemies list now extended to immigrants, particularly Jews and Catholics, seen as diluting the white Anglo-Saxon "dominant" American class.

This mix of anti-Blackness, anti-Semitism, nativism, and Protestant supremacy played out in events from the 1915 lynching of Leo Frank to the anti-Black Red Summer riots of 1919, stirring up white resentment and grievance to swell the Klan's ranks. It found converts in big cities and small towns alike, boasting a membership of anywhere from two to five million. The Second Klan ran members for elected office. They held open-air rallies and marches, extolling ideals of patriotism and drawing in a broad cross section of everyday white America: from farmers to educators to factory workers. There was at least one documented account of a Klan chapter in the United States Navy.

Bill draws on this real-life history of racial terror to tell a story that is at once grand in scope and personal. *The Day the Klan Came to Town* recounts happenings that took place in 1923 in his own hometown of Carnegie, Pennsylvania. While the Second Klan attempted to pass itself off as a normalized political entity in parts of the South and East, in the Midwest the old tactics of terror and mobocracy remained its key calling card. As one Pennsylvania Klan official of the time boasted of recruitment, "It takes riots to swell the ranks."

The planned terrorizing of Carnegie was to take place by way of a march through the mostly Irish-Catholic enclave of the town, aided and abetted by the local police chief—himself possibly a Klan member. But things didn't go exactly as planned. The intended victims of Carnegie weren't cowed. Instead, they came out and showed up to confront their harassers. To quote the sarcastic meme: "So much for the tolerant Left!"

The intended Klan riot and show of force turned into a Klan rout, as local citizens blocked roads and bridges, pelted the hooded marchers, and fought them in hand to hand melees. This was not the only moment of such resistance at the time. During the infamous Red Summer, Black veterans returning from World War I and other African Americans created armed defense units to protect their communities from rampaging white violence. Rosa Parks recalled at the age of six seeing her own grandfather brandishing a shotgun on their porch. "I stayed awake many nights, keeping vigil with Grandpa," she recounted. "I wanted to see him kill a Ku Kluxer. He declared the first to invade our home would surely die."

Bill spent time painstakingly researching the events in his hometown. Working with the Historical Society of Carnegie, he utilized old maps, topographic charts, and contemporary accounts to recreate the fateful and bloody confrontation. Artist Bizhan Khodabandeh brings this drama vividly to life with moving images that travel fluidly back and forth through time, linking together a vignette of experiences that tie back to the story's centralizing moment.

In this retelling, Carnegie is home to a diversity of people: Irish and African American, Jewish and Italian, all uniting in common cause against a common enemy. Many are immigrants, drawn to American shores with a promise of freedom—only to experience many of the harsh realities of inequality and oppression that "the shining city upon a hill" offered. It was a stark baptism that African Americans, who quite involuntarily arrived much earlier on those same shores, had long known and endured. The immigrants of Carnegie in Bill's story bring similar stories of tragedies and struggles against authoritarians and creeping fascism in their mother countries. In their imperfections, aspirations, and dreams, they are quintessentially more American—at least the America espoused through ideals—than the nativist and racist mob that seeks to destroy them. In their valiant defense of those rights, and the very right to exist as human beings, they are more patriotic than the fascists in hoods who wrap themselves in flags and carry the cross.

But if this is a story of past events, it also harkens to our present, where the white supremacy we'd thought banished to the periphery again seems ascendant. And we are left to ponder *The Day the Klan Came to Town* as it serves as a lesson for those of us looking for histories of resistance as we face this age-old enemy.

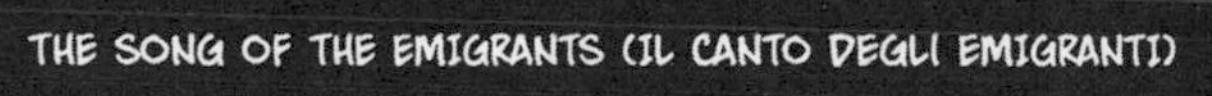

THE SONG OF THE EMIGRANTS (IL CANTO DEGLI EMIGRANTI)

WOLVES HAVE WARMED THEMSELVES ON OUR FLEECE AND EATEN OUR FLESH.
WE ARE THE GENERATION OF SHEEP.
WOLVES HAVE SHEARED US TO THE BONE WHILE WE PROTESTED ONLY TO GOD.
IN TIME OF PEACE WE SICKENED IN HOSPITALS OR JAILS
IN TIME OF WAR WE WERE CANNON FODDER.
WE HARVESTED BALES OF GRASS. ONE BLADE FOR US. THE REST FOR THE WOLVES.
ONE DAY A RUMOR SPREAD – THERE WAS A VAST AND DISTANT LAND
WHERE WE COULD LIVE MENO MALE.
SOME SHEEP WENT AND RETURNED. TRANSFORMED NO LONGER SHEEP
BUT WOLVES AND THEY ASSOCIATED WITH OUR WOLVES.
"WE WANT TO GO TO THAT VAST AND DISTANT COUNTRY," WE SHEEP SAID.
"WE WANT TO GO."
"THERE IS AN OCEAN TO CROSS," THE WOLVES SAID.
"WE WILL CROSS IT."
"AND IF YOU ARE SHIPWRECKED AND DROWNED?"
"IT'S BETTER TO DIE QUICKLY THAN SUFFER A LIFETIME."
"THERE ARE DISEASES ..."
"NO DISEASE CAN BE MORE HORRIBLE THAN HUNGER FROM FATHER TO SON."
AND THE WOLVES SAID, "SHEEP, THERE WILL BE DECEIVERS ..."
"YOU'VE BEEN DECEIVING US FOR CENTURIES."
"WOULD YOU ABANDON THE LAND OF YOUR FATHERS, YOUR BROTHERS?"
"YOU WHO FLEECE US ARE NOT OUR BROTHERS. THE LAND OF OUR FATHERS
IS A SLAUGHTERHOUSE."
IN TATTERS, IN GREAT HERDS WE IN PAIN BEYOND BELIEF JOURNEYED TO
THE VAST AND DISTANT LAND.
SOME OF US DID DROWN.
SOME OF US DID DIE OF PRIVATION
BUT FOR EVERY TEN THAT PERISHED A THOUSAND SURVIVED AND ENDURED.
BETTER TO CHOKE IN THE OCEAN THAN BE STRANGLED BY MISERY.
BETTER TO DECEIVE OURSELVES THAN BE DECEIVED BY THE WOLVES.
BETTER TO DIE IN OUR WAY THAN TO BE LOWER THAN THE BEASTS.

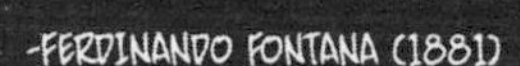

-FERDINANDO FONTANA (1881)

HOOooooo!
HOOOOO!
HOOoo!

THUD

HUFF
HUFF

NOW, FELLAS, HERE WE ARE, OUT ON A COON HUNT, AND WE DONE CAUGHT US A GUINEA INSTEAD.

CARNEGIE, PENNSYLVANIA. 1923

WHAT IS IT THIS TIME, CABBRIELI?

NOTHING, GIANNA.
IT'S NEVER "NOTHING."

YOU'RE STAYING HOME TONIGHT, RIGHT?
HMMPF.

THINK OF YOUR FAMILY, **CABBRIELI!**
I AM, VITA MIA.

The Day the Klan Came to Town

Written by Bill Campbell
Art by Bizhan Khodabandeh

COAL
COAL

YOU RAG PICKING, DITCH DIGGING, ORGAN GRINDER MONKEY CHASING, SACCO & VANZETTI ANARCHIST, PAGAN, POPE LOVING, KNIGHTS OF COLUMBUS, MUSTACHE PETE MAFIA ZIP, NEVER BE IRISH McARONI, "MANGIA! MANGIA!" MEATBALL FRYING, "NO SPEAKA DA ENGLISH," NAPPY HAIR, BIG NOSE, OLIVE OIL GREASEBALL, DAGO, WOP, GUINEA SPIC! GO THE HELL BACK TO ITALY!

CHAPTER 1

PITTSBURGH, PENNSYLVANIA 1923
BROTHERS! HELP YOURSELVES!
TONIGHT WE DEFEND AMERICA!
KKK
KNOCK KNOCK KNOCK

CHRIST H. KEISLING, AS I LIVE AND BREATHE! HOW CAN I HELP YOU?

THE BURGESS, CONLEY. HE'S AFRAID THERE'S GOING TO BE VIOLENCE TONIGHT.

WHY, NO. NOT FROM US.
THESE ARE FOR PROTECTION. AS YOU KNOW PERSONALLY, THE KLAN IS A PEACEFUL, CIVIC ORGANIZATION. YOU TELL THAT PAPIST NOT TO WORRY.
HEH HEH
HEH

HE SAYS YOU CAN'T MARCH INTO THE BOROUGH TONIGHT.
AND WHAT DO YOU SAY?
...

LOOK, CHRIST, YOU GO TELL **THAT CATHOLIC** THAT THE KLAN IS AN ORDINARILY PEACEFUL DEFENDER OF WHITE PROTESTANT MORALITY. WE ARE SIMPLY EXERCISING OUR FIRST AMENDMENT RIGHTS. WHAT RED-BLOODED AMERICAN CAN BE AGAINST **THAT?**

I FORGOT, CARNEGIE DOESN'T HAVE MANY AMERICANS.
YOU GOT NEGROES AND IRISH, JEWS, AND HUNKIES. CHINAMEN!
EVEN HEAR YOU GOT ARABS AND STARVING ARMENIANS!
WHERE DID ALL THE GOOD WHITE PEOPLE GO?
YOU GOT YOURSELVES SO MANY MONGRELS IN THAT TOWN, THAT'S NOT AMERICA. HELL, IT PROBABLY REEKS LIKE A KENNEL!
MAYBE SOMEBODY NEEDS TO GO DOWN THERE AND WASH ALL THAT SHIT INTO THE RIVER.
CPD

WHAT DID HE SAY, CHIEF?

I THINK WE'VE COME TO AN ... AGREEMENT.

PRIMO!

ALL THE TROUBLE WE WENT THROUGH TO GET TO AMERICA AND *THIS* IS WHAT YOU WANT TO DO?
THE IRISH WANT TO TALK, GIANNA. THAT IS ALL. I DON'T WANT TO DO ANYTHING. BUT WE MAY NOT HAVE A CHOICE.

WHO *LOOKS* FOR A QUARREL, FINDS A QUARREL, GABBRIELE...

CLICK

COMU SEMU?
MU SCUDDCI.
HA!

HEY, PRIMO. HEARD YOU WASN'T COMING. BUT WHEN FUGAZY SAID YOU WERE, I FIGURED I'D COME ALONG, TOO. HEAR WHAT PADDY HAS TO SAY.

I'M HERE, GIANNA IS WITH CHILD, AND I DON'T WANT TO FIGHT. BUT I AM HERE.

DON'T NOBODY WANNA FIGHT, FRIEND. SOMETIMES A MAN AIN'T GOT NO CHOICE.
WE HAULED OUTTA BAM TO GET AWAY FROM THESE OFAYS. NOW THEY UP HERE CAUSIN' TROUBLE. YOU CAN ASK GRANNY GRUNT. SOME OF US ARE READY.

MAYBE THEY WILL HAVE THEIR "KARNEGIE DAY" AND LEAVE, DOX.
IT NEVER WORKS THAT WAY, FUGAZY.
NO, IT DOES NOT.

HEY, GENTS!
GEORGE WASHINGTON YEE! WHAT YOU KNOW GOOD?

WHAT ARE YOU DOING HERE?

MY FATHER USED TO WORK ON A SUGAR PLANTATION IN LOUISIANA.

WE KNOW ALL ABOUT THE KU KLUX KLAN.

ICH WAR NIE EIN VERRÄTER.
ICH HABE AMERIKA GELIEBT!

CHAPTER 2

RACALMUTO, SICILY. 1915.

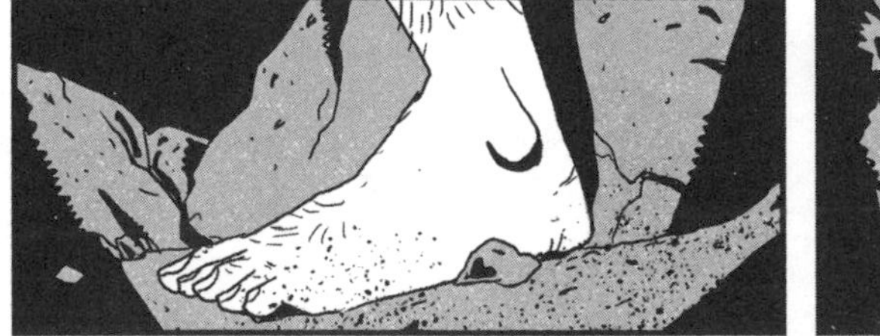

AH, LOOK AT CABBRIELE! ALL PRETTIED UP FOR THE MINE!
HEEHEE

MUST BE FROM HIS AMORE, CATENA.
THAT IS ONE WHITE-BREAD GIRL!

IT WAS PROBABLY FROM HER LITTLE SISTER.
BASTA, PIU!... IT WASN'T FROM GIANNA. CATENA GAVE IT TO ME HERSELF.

SCIURI, SCIURI, SCIURI, ♪♫ DI TUTTU L'ENNU! ♪♪ L'AMURI, CA MI DASTI TI LU TORNU!
TOLD YOU, RUSSO. THE MULIGNAN LOVES TO SING. THEY'RE GIFTED...

... LIKE MONKEYS.

CHE PALLE! WHAT DID THAT CAGOIA SAY?!
IT'S OK, MARCU...WHAT DO YOU WANT, VOLPE?

ME? WANT? IT'S NOT WHAT I WANT AT ALL. BUT WHAT OUR COUNTRY NEEDS...
HERE WE HAVE REAL MEN, REAL ITALIANI, DYING ON THE FRONT. FOR RELIGIONE. FOR PATRIA. FIGHTING OFF THE HUNS AND GOTHS LIKE THE EMPIRE OF OLD! WHILE YOU CARUSI SIT AROUND SINGING WITH YOUR ONION BREATH.

ITALIAN?! WE'RE FROM SCIACCI!
YEAH! DID THE MADONNA DEL SOCCORSO PICK UP HER CLUB TO FIGHT FOR YOUR KING?

MY FATHER WAS FASCI SICILIANI. HE FOUGHT FOR YOUR RISORGIMENTO. FOR YOUR ITALY. BUT AS SOON AS THE PADRONE GAVE THE WORD, YOU SUPERBI CAME DOWN FROM THE NORTH AND KILLED ALL THE PAESANI YOU COULD. INCLUDING MY FATHER!

YOU KNOW WHAT YOU CAN DO WITH YOUR PRECIOUS ITALY.
OH, WE'LL SEE ABOUT THAT, FANTINO.

♫ VIVE IL RE! VIVE IL RE! ♫
LE TROMBE LIETE SQUILLANO!
♫ ♪ ♪
SORRY, PAESANI. WHO KNEW THERE WAS A DRAFT?

CARNEGIE, PENNSYLVANIA. 1923
O LORD, HAVE MERCY ON US, FOR IN THEE HAVE WE PUT OUR TRUST. DO NOT BE ANGRY WITH US, NOR REMEMBER OUR INIQUITIES, BUT LOOK DOWN ON US EVEN NOW, SINCE THOU ART COMPASSIONATE, AND DELIVER US FROM OUR ENEMIES. FOR THOU ART OUR GOD, AND WE ARE THY PEOPLE; WE ARE ALL THE WORK OF THY HANDS, AND WE CALL ON THY NAME.
NOW AND EVER AND UNTO AGES OF AGES. AMEN.
AMEN.
AMEN.

AMEN.
AMEN.
AMEN.

THANK YOU, FATHER.

WHO IS THAT?
I HAVE NO IDEA.

FOR THOSE OF YOU WHO DO NOT KNOW ME, I AM THE BURGESS OF CARNEGIE BOROUGH, JOHN CONLEY.
LIKE MANY OF YOU, I AM CATHOLIC. BUT, MOST IMPORTANTLY, I AM AN AMERICAN. AND THESE ANIMALS WHO ARE COMING TODAY DO NOT REPRESENT AMERICA!
HA!

AMERICA IS A NATION OF LAWS! IT'S NOT RULED BY THE MOB AND WILL NOT BE TAKEN OVER BY TERRORISTS!
NOW, THE KLAN SAYS THEY'RE GOING TO MARCH THROUGH OUR BOROUGH, BUT I WILL NOT ALLOW IT. CHIEF KEISLING HAS GUARANTEED ME THAT OUR POLICE WILL NOT ALLOW IT.

HELL, THAT CRACKER PROBABLY INVITED THEM HERE.

VAFFANCULO, CAGOIA! YOU'RE **NOT** GOING TO STOP NOTHING!

THE CZAR USED TO MAKE SUCH PROMISES! AND NOW WE ARE HERE!
YEAH!
YEAH!

BALFASZ!!!
CHOOCH!!!
HAU AB!!!
GOBDAW!!!
STUPID ASS PECKERWOOD!!!
CHENT!!!

THIS DAY COULDN'T GET ANY WORSE.
DON'T LOOK UP THEN.

JESUS, MARY, AND JOSEPH ...

NOW SEE, BACK HOME IN KENTUCKY, YOU'RE STARTING TO SEE MILLS LIKE THESE POPPING UP. MINES, TOO. AND IT'S A DAMN SHAME.

WHEN I WAS GROWING UP, WE WERE FARMERS, BOY. PROUD, STRONG WHITE MEN WHO THRUST OUR HANDS IN THE SOIL AND CARVED OUT A TRULY GREAT NATION IN OUR OWN IMAGE!

BUT THESE MILLS, WITH **THEIR** "MODERNITY," ALL THEY BRING IS FILTH AND POLLUTION. THESE MICKS AND GUINEAS WITH **THEIR** ALCOHOL AND **DISEASE** –THEIR INFLUENZA AND SYPHILIS! THEY WILL **NEVER** BE **REAL** AMERICANS.

TONIGHT IS THE NIGHT WE SHOW THESE MONGRELS WHAT **AMERICANISM** TRULY MEANS.

SOME OF YALL KNOW ME. LOT MORE OF Y'ALL DON'T LIKE ME. IT'S LIKE THE FIRST WORD THEY TEACH YA OFF THE BOAT IS "NIGGER," BUT WE GONE PRETEND THAT DON'T MATTER TONIGHT.

I FOUGHT IN THE LAST WAR. MY DADDY **FOUGHT** IN THE WAR BEFORE THAT. HIS DADDY, THE WAR **BEFORE** THAT. NEGROES HAVE BEEN FIGHTIN' FOR THIS COUNTRY BEFORE IT WAS A COUNTRY. IF AMERICA **AIN'T** THE NEGRO'S COUNTRY, I DON'T KNOW WHOSE IT IS...
I'M TIRED A HAVIN' TO FIGHT FOR AMERICA AND MY PLACE IN IT. BUT IF THESE KU KLUXERS BE ITCHIN' FOR A FIGHT, WE GOT A SCRATCH THEY MIGHT NOT BE ABLE TO HANDLE.

THE CZAR, THE COSSACKS, THE WHITE ARMY, THE RED. **WE** JEWS ARE UNDER NO ILLUSION THAT WE HAVE A FRIEND IN THIS WORLD. BUT TONIGHT—WE ARE FRIENDS.

I AM ARMENIAN. THE ENTIRE WORLD STOOD BY AS MY PEOPLE WERE SLAUGHTERED...
FIRST IS THE NAME-CALLING. THEN THE INTIMIDATION AND BEATINGS. THEN EXPULSIONS...
IF THESE EARLY STAGES ARE MADE EASY FOR THEM, THEY WILL FIND THE FINAL STAGES EASIEST OF ALL.

THOSE WERE SOME HARSH WORDS, FREEMAN.
MR. CHARLIE GET HIS FEELINGS HURT?

I THANK **YOU,** ALMA THANKS YOU. BRIDGET AND JAMES WILL, TOO, WHEN THEVY'RE OLD ENOUGH.
TOLD MY SISTER YOU WAS TROUBLE, PADDY. YOU JUST LUCKY I WAS IN MARNE WHEN YOU PROPOSED.

AND THANK YOU FOR COMING, PRIMO. YOU COULD'VE SPOKEN, YOU KNOW? PEOPLE LISTEN TO YOU.

PEOPLE LISTEN TO MY PAESANO BECAUSE HE RARELY SPEAKS. THE MAN WHO TALKS A LOT SAYS NOTHING; THE MAN WHO TALKS LITTLE IS WISE.

I FEAR YOU'RE RIGHT, FUGAZY. I HOPE PEOPLE ARE READY.

CHE PALLE! EVERYBODY KNOWS WE HAVE A WAR ON OUR HANDS.

BUT GOV. PINCHOT, IF THIS ISN'T A TIME FOR THE NATIONAL GUARD, WHEN IS?!

DAMN REPUBLICANS ...
BURGESS CONLEY! GET A LOAD OF THIS.

YOU JACKASSES ARE IN THE UNITED STATES ARMY?!

CHAPTER 3

TOFANA DI ROZES, ITALY. "IL CASTELLETTO." 1915

OH ... PIU ...

PER LI SETTI BATTITURA
CHI PATÌ NOSTRU SIGNURI PI LI
CHIOVA ARRIBUCCATI ARMUZZI
SANTI, ARRIFRISCATI ...

YOU ARE NO LONGER DRUNKEN, LAZY PAESANI! YOU ARE ITALIANI! BOLD! STRONG! COURAGEOUS MEN! FIGHTING FOR RELIGIONE E PATRIA! YOU! DO! NOT! RUN!!!

FIRE!!!
BANG
BANG
BA-BANG

NOW ON TO GORIZIA!!!
FANTINO ...?

LUIGI ... DID WE—?
NO! WE WERE WAY OVER ON THE OTHER SIDE OF THE LINE.
BUT...
THE OTHER SIDE, GABBRIELE!!!

OK, LUIGI. OK...

SCIACCA, SICILY. 1920

CARO AMICO...
CABBRIELE.

WHAT HAS HAPPENED TO YOU?
THEIR WAR.
AND YOU HAVE NO WORK?

I TRIED, GIANNA. THE MINES...
ALL I SEE... NO. NO WORK.

I'M STAYING WITH LUIGI FOR NOW.
HE'S BACK IN THE MINES. I CAN'T
SEEM TO FIND MARCU.

OH, MY LITTLE COUSIN. HE'S AROUND. DOING ...
SOMETHING. SOME SAY HE'S WITH PRINCE PIETRO AND
PARTITO ECONOMICO. SOME, WITH THE SOCIALISTS.
OTHER SAY HE'S WITH THE FASCISTS.
FASCI SICILIANO?
NO! THE REAL
FASCISTS!

PARTITO NAZIONALE FASCISTA! LED BY IL DUCE, BENITO AMILCARE ANDREA MUSSOLINI! THE ONLY ONE WHO CAN TAKE THAT MAIMED VICTORY OF A WAR AND TURN IT INTO A REAL FASCIST TRIUMPH!!!

IMBOSCATO! WE ARE THE ONES WHO FOUGHT AND DIED IN THE TRENCHES WHILE COWARDS LIKE YOU STAYED BEHIND TO STEAL OUR WOMEN!
AH, CABBRIELI. DON'T BLAME ***ME*** THAT YOU LOST THAT PRETTY LITTLE SCARF OF YOURS AT GORIZIA.
MINCHIA!

GENTLEMEN, YOU ARE THE TRUE TRINCEROCRAZIA. NOT THIS "HERO" OF CAPORETTO.

SU, COMPAGNI IN FORTI SCHIERE, MARCIAM VERSO L'AVVENIRE!

HE WHO DIGS A GRAVE FOR HIS BROTHER FALLS IN IT HIMSELF.
NO, CABBRIELE. YOU MUST LEAVE. VOLPE IS MORE POWERFUL THAN YOU CAN IMAGINE.

THE SHIP IS ABOUT TO GO. YOU SHOULD LEAVE NOW.
THANK YOU, GIANNA.

REGNO D'ITALIA
PASSAPORTO
PER L'ESTERO
TAKE THESE.

WHERE DID YOU GET THESE?
NOTHING SCRATCHES MY HAND LIKE MY OWN NAILS.
HM.

WHO IS THIS "PRIMO SALERNO"?
SOMEBODY THE BLACKSHIRTS AREN'T LOOKING FOR—UNLIKE GABBRIELE PARISI.

BON VIAGGIU, PAESANO.

AMUNNINNI, "PRIMO"!
THE SHIP WILL NOT WAIT FOR US.

I THINK YOU DROPPED THIS.

LOVE IS LIKE A COUGH, LUIGI... IMPOSSIBLE TO HIDE.

CHAPTER 4

MARKO SKAČE, MARKO SKAČE PO ZELENOJ TRATI! AJ AJ, AJAJAJ! PO ZELENOJ TRAT!

V ROKAH NOSI, V ROKAH NOSI SEDEM ŽUTIH ZLATIH!
YOU DIDN'T HAVE TO COME, LUIGI.

AJ AJ, AJAJAJ!!!
YES, I DID. A MAN WITHOUT HIS PAESANI WILL HAVE NOTHING BUT TROUBLE THROUGHOUT HIS LIFE. AND WE ARE PAESANI.

PO ZELENI TRATI!
MALADITU LAMERICA E CHI LA SPRIMINTA.

NO, NO, NO. GOD BLESS AMERICA. YOU'VE HEARD THE STORIES. AMERICA IS PAVED WITH GOLD. WE SIMPLY GRAB OUR SHOVELS AND GET RICH!

THEN "PRIMO SALERNO" GOES BACK TO SCIACCA, SEES HIS GIANNA, "BEDDA VIENI QUA," AND FILLS HIS CASTLE WITH CUCCIOLI!!!

V ROKAH NOSI, V ROKAH NOSI SEDEM ŽUTIH ZLATIH!
AJ AJ, AJAJAJ!!!

E
FT
CT

WHAT IS TAKING SO LONG? WHY DO THEY HAVE LETTERS ON THEIR CLOTHES?
"X" IS FOR THE MENTALLY DEFICIENT. "B" IS FOR BACK PROBLEMS.

THEN THERE ARE LETTERS FOR CONJUNCTIVITIS, TRACHOMA, YOUR EYES AND FACE AND FEET, GOITER, HEART, HERNIA, LAMENESS, NECK, LUNGS, PREGNANCY, AND EVEN SENILITY.

YOU ITALIANS CALL THIS PLACE "THE ISLAND OF TEARS." HALF OF THESE PEOPLE WILL GET RIGHT BACK ON THAT BOAT.

THEY NEED US, BUT THEY DO NOT WELCOME US.

NEW ORLEANS, LOUISIANA. 1921

COLORED ONLY

AND HERE YOU ARE, PINING FOR GIANNA AGAIN. DON'T WORRY, PAESANO. MUSSOLINI'S DAYS ARE NUMBERED AND YOU CAN GO BACK. OR BETTER YET, YOU CAN BRING GIANNA HERE!

BUT, LUIGI-
NIGGERS!!!

RUN!!!

KNOCK
KNOCK

YOU'VE GOT A LETTER, SALERNO. FROM PENNSYLVANIA?

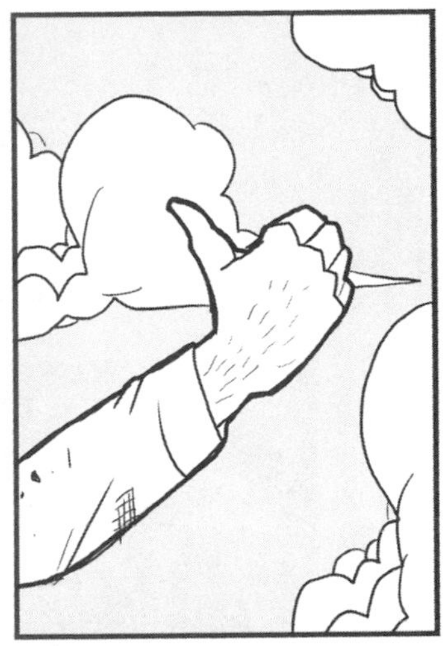

KNOCK
KNOCK

MINCHIA!

CABBRIELE!!!
TI VUGGHIU BINI ...

CHAPTER 5

FREEMAN, YOU EVER KNOW FEAR?

GROWIN' UP IN BAM? EVERY DAY OF MY LIFE. IN VERDUN, EVERY SECOND. BUT YOU KNOW ALL ABOUT THAT, DON'T YOU?

YES. I DO. EVERY DAY PEOPLE LIKE YOU AND ME ARE ASKED TO FIGHT, AND EVERY DAY WE DIE. WHY IS TODAY ANY DIFFERENT?

LOOK, PAESANO. DO I LOVE LAMERICA? I DON'T KNOW, YET. WHAT I *DO* KNOW IS, WHEN I GO TO THE MINE, I DO SO WITH MY CLOTHES ON AND MY SHOULDERS HIGH. I DO NOT DO WHAT I HAD TO DO IN SCIACCA TO SURVIVE.
I DO NOT STARVE ON BREAD AND SARDINES—BUT FEAST ON BUCATTINI, LA BIF STEKA, AND LA CHICKEN.

ONE DAY, I WILL FIND A WOMAN AS GOOD AS MY COUSIN, AND WE WILL RAISE A FAMILY. I WAS NOT ABLE TO DO THAT IN SICILY, BUT I CAN DO IT HERE. NO ONE WILL TAKE THAT AWAY FROM ME. CAPISCIU?

HOPEFULLY, IT WON'T COME TO THAT, YOUNGUN.

THIS COUNTRY AIN'T AS GREAT AS ADVERTISED. THAT'S FOR DAMN SURE. BUT I GOT KIDS, TOO, AND I GOTTA BELIEVE BETTER DAYS IS AHEAD.
...SOMETIMES YOU GOTTA FIGHT FOR THEM DAYS. FOR THE COUNTRY YOU WANT YOUR KIDS AND THEY KIDS TO GROW UP IN.
...LOOKIN' LIKE TODAY MIGHT JUST BE ONE OF THEM DAYS.

EXALTED CYCLOPS MCNEEL, PARADE MARSHALL BARCLAY. WHY, IT LOOKS LIKE KARNEGIE DAY IS A SMASHING SUCCESS.

THE BAND IS **FANTASTIC!**

YOUNG LOVE FLOURISHING!

FAMILIES TOGETHER, **ENJOYING THIS BEAUTIFUL DAY!**

NOW, THIS, **GENTLEMEN**, IS WHAT AMERICA IS ALL ABOUT!

IT LOOKS LIKE WE'LL HAVE ABOUT 30,000 FOR TODAY'S KONKLAVE, GRAND WIZARD.
AND EVERYONE IS ARMED? I GAVE ALL MY FIREARMS AWAY.

I CAN'T SPEAK FOR EVERYBODY, BUT ARMSTRONG COUNTY IS READY. THE GOOD FOLKS OF WEST VIRGINIA AND KENTUCKY WON'T DISAPPOINT, I'M SURE.

EXCELLENT. NOW HERE'S THE LIST, BARCLAY.
CROSS BURNINGS, RIOTS, AND THE LIKE ARE FUN, BUT NOTHING SWELLS THE RANKS LIKE A MARTYR. THESE 15 MEN ARE WILLING TO HELP THE CAUSE.

THANK YOU, SIR. AND THE MARCH ITSELF?
THE POLICE CHIEF AND I HAVE COME TO AN UNDERSTANDING, IF YOU WILL.

NOW, WOULD YOU LOOKY HERE?

GENTLEMEN, CHILDREN TRULY ARE THE FUTURE. I HAVE HOPE FOR THIS COUNTRY, YET.

PHEW...

MRS. PAGANI, I HAVE TO DELIVER THESE SHIRTS TO MR. YEE. BUT I DON'T WANT TO BE ALONE WITH ALL THESE PEOPLE IN TOWN.
WHY? THEY AREN'T AFTER YOU.

BUT MR. FREEMAN SAYS THEY HATE US BECAUSE WE ARE CATHOLIC. THEY SAY WE ARE NOT CHRISTIAN.
FREEMAN?! BOH! YOU KNOW NOT TO TRUST ANYTHING A MULIGNAN SAYS.

CLICK!
CLICK!
CLICK!
YOU'LL BE FINE, RAGAZZINA!

LITTLE JIMMY IS SIMPLY OBSESSED WITH PIE TRAYNOR.
BETTER THAN THAT KRAUT, WAGNER. I HEAR HE'S FROM HERE.
FIGURES. ... JAGOFF.

HEY!!!

DON'T YOU DAGOS KNOW TO CLEAR THE SIDEWALK WHEN WHITE WOMEN ARE WALKING IT?!

LADIES! CAN'T YOU SEE THIS POOR WOMAN'S CONDITION?!
OF COURSE WE CAN!

I'M SO SORRY, MA'AM. YOU KNOW, WE'RE NOT ALL LIKE THAT.
YES, YES. OF COURSE NOT.

IT'S JUST THAT OUR FOREFATHERS SACRIFICED A LOT TO MAKE THIS LAND GREAT. IT WOULD BE *TRAGIC* TO SEE IT FALL INTO THE WRONG HANDS.

THOUGH YOURS ARE QUITE SOFT.

BY THE WAY, MY NAME I-
AHEM!!!

SPADAJ, LOVER BOY! YOU HAVE DONE QUITE ENOUGH HERE.

UNBELIEVABLE!!!
0
9
8
7
6
5
4
3
2
1

NOBODY WANTS TO HELP US. YOU'D THINK ALL OF PENNSYLVANIA WANTS TO SEE THE KLAN BURN CARNEGIE TO THE GROUND.

IN ALL FAIRNESS, BURGESS CONLEY, THE MODERN KU KLUX KLAN IS A CIVIC ORGANIZATION. THEY'RE HERE TO SIMPLY EXERCISE THEIR FIRST AMENDMENT RIGHTS.
CPD
CPD

THE MER ROUGE MURDERS?! THEY RAN THOSE NEGROES OUT OF TOWN UP IN BEAVER AND KIDNAPPED ANOTHER ONE. AND A CHILD WAS KIDNAPPED IN EAST LIBERTY!

I DON'T KNOW ABOUT ALL THAT. I'M JUST SAYING THE KLAN HAS A LOT MORE SYMPATHIZERS THAN YOU **MAY THINK.**
CPD
CPD

ALL I'M SAYING, CHIEF KEISLING, IS CARNEGIE BETTER BE PREPARED.
OH, WE KNOW EXACTLY WHAT TO DO.

A LITTLE MORE!...
A LITTLE MORE!

PERFECT!
BUMP!

NOBODY'S GETTING THROUGH HERE.
PADDY!!!

WHAT IS IT, STUSH?
OLD MAN MACVEIGH LOANED US HIS JALOPY, BUT THAT'S ALL WE COULD GET FOR THE GLENDALE BRIDGE.

AH, THAT'S IRISH TOWN. NO CÚL TÓNA'S THICK ENOUGH TO COME OUR WAY.
BUT IF THEY DO, WE'LL BE READY FOR THEM

ÁVE MARÍA, GRÁTIA PLÉNA, DÓMINUS TÉCUM. BENEDÍCTA TU IN MULIÉRIBUS, ET BENEDÍCTUS FRÚCTUS VÉNTRIS TÚI, IÉSUS SÁNCTA MARÍA, MÁTER DÉI, ÓRA PRO NÓBIS PECCATÓRIBUS, NUNC ET IN HÓRA MÓRTIS NÓSTRAE.
AMEN.
CHAPTER 6

HURRAH!
HURRAH!
HURRAH!

PERFECT!
HURRAH!
HURRAH!
HURRAH!

WHEN IRISH EYES ARE SMILING
SURE, 'TIS LIKE THE MORN IN SPRING
♪ IN THE LILT OF IRISH LAUGHTER ♫
YOU CAN HEAR THE ANGELS SING ...

YOUR BOY FUGAZY SURE DOES PICK A **MEAN** GUITAR.
SALVATORE? HE IS A MAN OF MANY TALENTS.

SO... YOU GOOD, PRIMO?

YES, FREEMAN... I AM "GOOD."

I GOTCHA, PRIMO. MAYBE WE SHOULD HOPE FOR THE BEST HERE. THAT FELLA MOSHE'S PLANNED A LITTLE "WELCOME TO CARNEGIE" FOR THEM CRACKERS.
HEY, ENDA! WHAT ELSE YOU GOT, ANAM CARA?!

MY LORD CALLS ME, HE CALLS ME THE THUNDER;
THE TRUMPET SOUNDS IT IN MY SOUL,
♪♫ I HAIN'T GOT LONG TO STAY HERE. ♪♪
STEAL AWAY, STEAL AWAY, STEAL AWAY TO JESUS!

I AM SO SORRY, MARTA. I DID NOT MEAN TO SLEEP SO LONG.

PROSZE, IN YOUR CONDITION? YOU NEED SLEEP. AND FOOD.

SMELLS WONDERFUL.
FASOLKA PO BRETONSKU. YES. IT HAS EVERYTHING YOU NEED IN LIFE.

THANK YOU FOR YOUR KINDNESS, BUT I SHOULD BE GOING HOME SOON.
NO, CHILD. IT IS TOO DANGEROUS.
A CHURCH THEN? THEY PROVIDE SANCTUARY.

THE IRISH CHURCH WON'T EVEN BAPTIZE AN ITALIAN BABY. THEY WON'T TAKE YOU IN. THE GERMAN CHURCH ISN'T MUCH BETTER. MAYBE THE POLAK CHURCH, BUT YOU'LL NEVER MAKE IT UP THE HILL.

NO. YOU STAY HERE WITH ME. WE'RE IN IRISH TOWN. WE WILL BE SAFE HERE.

DO NOT FORGET, MOSHE.
I KNOW, I KNOW, YITZHAK...

ONLY A WARNING SHOT.

WELCOME TO ALL YOU FINE KLAVERNS, KLEAGLES, AND KLIGRAPPS—YOU GLORIOUS MEN, WOMEN, AND CHILDREN—AND THE ONE THOUSAND NEW MEMBERS OF THE KU KLUX KLAN, *THE HEROES OF AMERICA!!!*

HURRAH!!!!!

TONIGHT, ALL OF AMERICA WILL KNOW WHAT WE HAVE DONE HERE! PROTECTING OUR FRAGILE CONSTITUTION AND THIS PRECIOUS COUNTRY FROM THE MONGREL HORDES WHO BRING PESTILENCE AND WAR TO OUR SHORES!!!
...NO MORE NIGGERS! NO MORE SHEENIES! NO MICKS! NO WOPS OR CHINKS! WE SAY NO!!! AMERICA IS NOT FOR THEM!
...AMERICA IS FOR AMERICANS!!!

NOW, PUT YOUR HANDS TOGETHER FOR OUR MAGNIFICENT LEADER, THE IMPERIAL WIZARD HIRAM! WESLEY! EVANS!!!

DER KOP ZOL IM AROP...

HURRAH! HURRAH!

BANG

THONK

GO! GO! GO!

HA! SEEMS LIKE THE MONGRELS GOT A LITTLE YELP IN 'EM. TONIGHT, WE'LL SHOW 'EM HOW A *REAL* DOG *BITES!!!*

ONWARD CHRISTIAN SOLDIERS!
MARCHING AS TO WAR,
WITH THE CROSS OF JESUS
GOING ON BEFORE ....

LIKE A MIGHTY ARMY
MOVES THE CHURCH OF GOD:
BROTHERS, WE ARE TREADING
WHERE THE SAINTS HAVE TROD;
WE ARE NOT DIVIDED,
ALL ONE BODY WE—
ONE IN FAITH AND SPIRIT,
ONE ETERNALLY!
RED UP THIS TOWN!
GIVE 'EM HELL, BOYS!!!
WE LOVE YOU!
KKK

NINNA NANNA MARINARE
'NGOPP A VARCA, MIEZO O MARE
LO TE PARL E NUN RESPUNN
TE SI PERZE MIEZ O SUONN ...

PADDY! THEY'RE MARCHING DOWN WASHINGTON AVENUE TOWARD CAROTHERS! THERE'S THOUSANDS OF 'EM! THEY'RE HEADED FOR IRISH TOWN!
FECKERS! LET'S GO, BOYS!

BURGESS! THE KLAN'S ON THE MOVE! LOOKS LIKE IRISH TOWN'S THE TARGET! THERE'S ALREADY A BUNCH OF BOG TROTTERS THERE ARMED AND READY!
DID YOU-?!
AH, HELL!

C'MON, MEN!!!

HURRY IT UP THERE, FINN! THE BASTARDS ARE ALMOST HERE!
ALL RIGHT, KENNY! I NEED MORE BUCKETS!

THE RUSSIANS KILLED MY HUSBAND IN ŁÓDŹ DURING THE REVOLUTION. THE SOVIETS MURDERED MY ANDRZEJ THREE YEARS AGO. I HA–

GASP MARTA, *GASP* THE KLAN IS COMING THIS WAY!

ARE THE OTHERS ON THE ROOF?
YEAH. THEY–
YOU **CANNOT** LEAVE ME BEHIND!

OH, WE'LL BE RIGHT BACK, DARLING. YOU WILL BE SAFE HERE.
I AM FROM SCIACCA. IF YOU FIGHT, I WILL FIGHT,.

HUFF HUFF THEN SHE WILL FIGHT, TOO.

ONWARD, THEN, YE PEOPLE!
JOIN OUR HAPPY THRONG
KKK
BLEND WITH OURS YOUR VOICES IN THE TRIUMPH SONG.

ARE YOU READY, CHIEF?
MORE THAN YOU KNOW, BURGESS.
GLORY, LAUD AND HONOR UNTO CHRIST, THE KING; THIS THROUGH COUNTLESS AGES MEN AND ANGELS SING.

WHAT'S GOING ON?
I HAVE NO IDEA.

WHAT THE HELL KIND OF NONSENSE ARE YA *TALKING* ABOUT, BARCLAY?!

SIMPLE, BURGESS CONLEY. YOU SAY WE DON'T HAVE A PERMIT TO MARCH, BUT THE BUROUGH OF CARNEGIE DOESN'T ISSUE SUCH PERMITS.

RIGHT! WHICH MEANS YOU CAN'T MARCH.
ACCORDING TO PENNSYLVANIA LAW, IT MEANS YOU CAN'T LEGALLY STOP US FROM MARCHING. YOU WOULD BE IMPEDING OUR RIGHTS TO FREE SPEECH.

ISN'T THAT RIGHT, CHIEF KEISLING?

SORRY, BURGESS. IT WOULD BE ILLEGAL TO STOP THEM.
I'M THE CHIEF OF POLICE. I AM HERE TO ENFORCE THE LAW. I CAN'T BE BREAKING IT, NOW COULD I?

JESUS, MARY, AND JOSEPH!

LET 'EM THROUGH!

KKK

FAG AN BHEALACH!!
KKK

GET 'EM!
AAAH!!!
LAVET KUNEM!!!

KKK

LET'S TEACH THESE MUTTS A LESSON!!!

GIVE IT TO THEM, LADIES!!!

BANG
BLAM

MARTA! YOU'VE BEEN SHOT!
THEN I WILL THROW WITH MY RIGHT.

OH, NO YOU DON'T, MISS ANNE!

COME GIT YO'S, FELLAS!!!

GOT YOUR BACK, PRIMO, IF YOU GOT MINE.

CABBRIELE.
WHAT?
MY NAME IS CABBRIELE. NOT "PRIMO." YOU ARE MY FRIEND. YOU SHOULD KNOW.

WELL, ALL RIGHT THEN. I GOT YOUR BACK, FRIEND.

AND I HAVE YOURS. A MAN WITHOUT HIS FRIENDS WILL HAVE NOTHING BUT TROUBLE THROUGHOUT HIS LIFE.

AAAAAAAAAHHHH!!!
FINN!!!
AAAAH!!!

WE'RE OUT OF BRICKS AND COAL.
DIRTY KIKE!

I THINK WE'RE DONE FOR, PADDY.
THEY WILL NOT WIN TONIGHT!
DAMN OFAYS...

RUN, PUTTANIERE.
CABBRIELE!!!
MARCU?!!!

GO! SAVE MARCU!
BUT Y–
I'M FINE! GO! NOW!
BASTA ...
BLAM!

TOMMY?!!!

THEY KILLED TOMMY!!!

THEY'VE GOT GUNS. IT'S TIME WE VAMOOSE, BOYS!

LET'S GO. LET'S GO.

PRYČ, KORVA!!!

SHHH...

HA! HA!!! YOU COULD'VE STOPPED ALL THIS, KEISLING! BUT YOU DIDN'T! AND YOUR KU KLUX CLOWNS GOT THEIR ASSES KICKED!!!

KISS MY IRISH ASS, YOU KRAUT BASTARD!!!

FELLAS, FELLAS.
I'LL BE ALL RIGHT.
CABBRIELE?!!!

BEDDA VIENI QUA!

AHHH... RIMBABAMBITO...
TI VUGGHIU BINI.

PEOPLE WILL REMEMBER WHAT WE DID HERE TONIGHT.
NAW, MARCU...

WE AMERICANS LOVE FORGETTING. IT'S HOW WE KEEP DOIN' WHAT WE DO.

ICE
POLICE
ICE
POLICE
ICE
POLICE
I WAS BORN HERE.

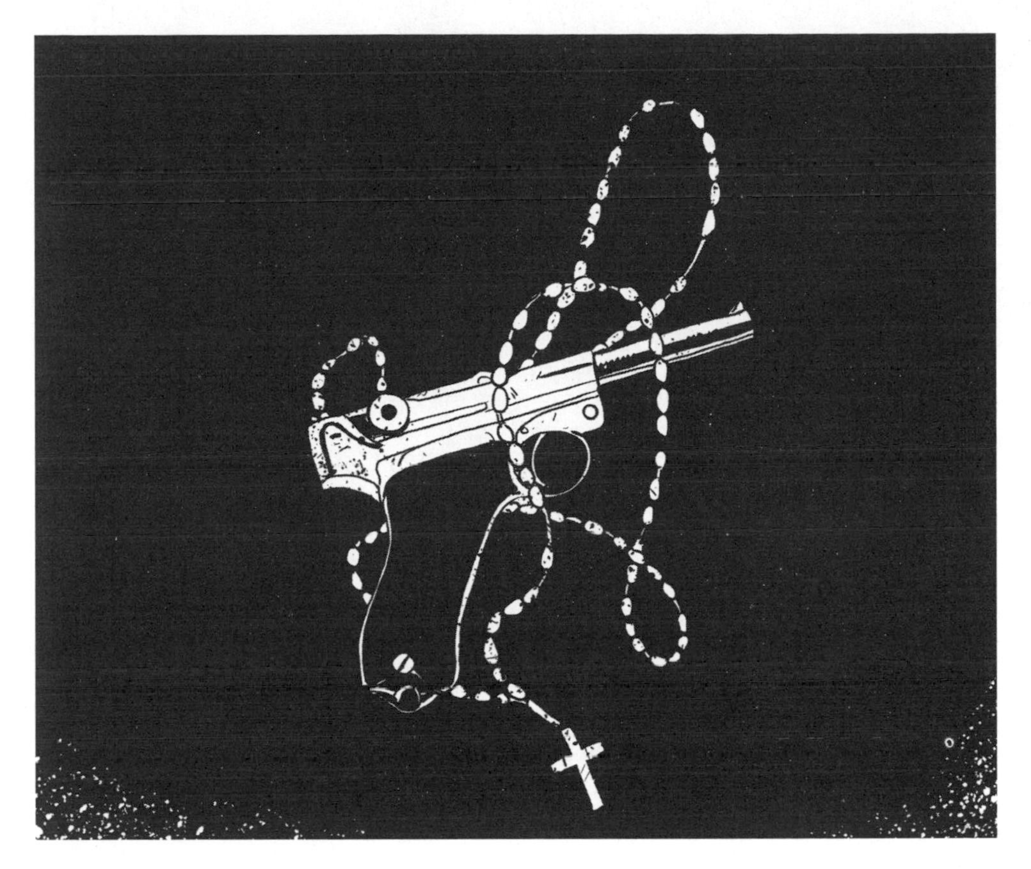

Afterword

By Bill Campbell

Yeah, yeah, yeah. We all know the old saying "History is written by the victors." I was a bit of a history nerd growing up. I knew that old quote, but the ramifications of it didn't hit me until much later, when I found the writings of Vincent Harding and Howard Zinn. It was only then that I started to understand that the thing I was taught in school wasn't history as much as it was American fanfic. That was when I became less interested in what the "victors" had written, but what they continue to leave out.

The Day the Klan Came to Town is one such story. The immigrants in this story are indeed the victors. They beat the Klan that day and won in their ultimate goal of kicking the Klan out of Pennsylvania a century ago. But they won an even larger victory. They ultimately became "white" and, as a result, became the beneficiaries of all that whiteness has to offer in this country.

Once you're admitted into any club, you want to act as though you've always been a member. So it's no surprise that this story has largely gone untold, especially as the language of many of the people here and their descendants—such as Carnegie native Mike Ditka, born "Dyczko"—has grown to resemble that of the people who originally didn't want them in the US.

My family moved to Carnegie in 1978. I grew up there. The church on the cover is the old steeple of the Catholic church I attended. That Klansman was killed in front of that church. Yet neither I nor anyone I grew up with had ever heard about any of this.

A good friend of mine, comics creator Jiba Molei Anderson, often says that "whiteness is erasure." Countless European cultural folkways, traditions, and attitudes have actually eventually been washed away upon coming to these shores in order for folks to be considered "white." This exchange has been rewarded with material gain, obviously. This affords many a convenient amnesia and a convenient narrative of how America has always greeted immigrants with open arms (and this latest wave is somehow different), how they worked hard to get what they have, that all other people have to do is work hard, and so on, when really all that happened was they were granted "whiteness" and different forms of discrimination were removed from their paths.

But as Sportin' Life sang in *Porgy and Bess*, it ain't necessarily so. As a writer, an amateur history buff, and a Black man who grew up in this "white" town, it is with Sportin's glee that I wrote this story in order to hopefully make you question what you've learned in America's "good book."

As I have noted, this is largely forgotten history. Research wasn't easy. A chapter or two in a monograph here and there, a brief mention in some old articles. Oddly enough, the actions of the Klan and government officials that day have been chronicled. All we really know about the people who fought them is that they were "Irish and others."

So this is a fictionalized account of an actual historical event. The Klansmen, the mayor, and the police chief are all real. Primo and his gang are not—with the notable exception of George Washington Lee, who was actually about nine years old at the time (I just loved his name and had to include him). While Primo's story is largely made-up, it was heavily researched. I not only wanted to get it as "right" as I could as an outsider, but I also wanted his to be, to the best of my ability, a Sicilian immigrant story. What happened to Primo very likely happened to many in his position. It's a story not unlike what many people experience today in their searches for a better life. I feel it's a story worth telling over and over until people no longer choose to forget what others go through.

Acknowledgments

Bill Campbell

First and foremost, I have to thank my wife and kids, who deserve combat pay for having to deal with a husband and father who's also a writer and publisher. Believe me, they put up with a lot. Thanks also go to my brother, Gerald Mohamed, for out-history-nerding me and telling me about this riot in the first place. I grew up in Carnegie and never heard about this. If it were up to me, they'd have an Anti-Klan Day every year. But these things are never up to me.

I owe a huge debt of gratitude to the Historical Society of Carnegie. I was a bit apprehensive about going to them for this (after all, it must be a town secret for a reason), but my God were they helpful! We pored over old maps and photos, found some illustrations, looked through some old writing, speculated on so many things. We even found the original Carnegie *Klan* charter (yep, they got their own a year after the riot) and even found their listing in a 1924 phone book (listed under SECRET SOCIETIES—you can't make this shit up).

Thanks to Minh Le for his help with Vietnamese and Ben Rosenbaum for the Yiddish. Also, big thanks to Karen Haas, who dug up Carnegie's census data so we could figure out who actually lived in the town and who likely participated in the riot. The town was a bit more diverse and less segregated than I had originally imagined.

Last but by no means least, thanks to my partner in crime, Bizhan Khodabandeh. When the idea for Klan popped into my head, it did so with Bizhan's art. I was ecstatic when he agreed to work on this with me, and I remained thrilled with every page he drew. It's an honor and a privilege to work with the man, and nothing makes me happier than to call him my friend.

Bizhan Khodabandeh

Special thanks to Bill Campbell for thinking my work is good enough for such a project. Thanks for continuously being supportive of my work and even encouraging me when I lacked the confidence in it. I cherish the friendship we've built over the years. Also thanks for all the time spent researching visuals for me to make sure the work was accurate to the time and respective cultures.

Thanks to those who were willing to spend the time to read the book and provide us a statement for it. I am very humbled by those who were gracious enough to answer that call.

I'd like to also thank my family for being supportive of my work in many ways. Thanks to Kelly Alder and Tom De Haven for being willing to read the book in its early stages to provide any advice to me. I'd also like to thank my comics community in Richmond who I'm afraid to list because I know that I'll leave out some of them. You feel like a second family to me. For those I showed the process work to, thanks for being encouraging and supportive of it.

And of course, we both would like to thank PM Press! There aren't too many publishers with the courage to take a project like this on. They are truly an important fixture in the world taking on projects like this one.

Additional Art

Pictured below: concept sketches for Primo and page thumbnails for *The Day the Klan Came to Town*

Pictured right: Digital illustration by Bizhan Khodabandeh documenting some of the graffiti after BLM protests in Richmond, VA. Pictured is the Robert E. Lee Monument renamed the Marcus-David Peters Circle. Prints were sold to raise money for the Richmond Transparency and Accountability Project.

REVOLUTION
ACAB
STOP POLICE
BLM
LIVES

Biographies

Bill Campbell is the author of *Sunshine Patriots*; *My Booty Novel*; *Pop Culture: Politics, Puns, "Poohbutt" from a Liberal Stay-at-Home Dad*; *Koontown Killing Kaper*; and *Baaaad Muthaz*. Along with Edward Austin Hall, he coedited the groundbreaking anthology *Mothership: Tales from Afrofuturism and Beyond*. He has also coedited *Stories for Chip: A Tribute to Samuel R. Delany; APB: Artists against Police Brutality* (for which he won a Glyph Pioneer/Lifetime Achievement Award); and *Future Fiction: New Dimensions of International Fantasy and Science Fiction*. His latest anthology is a two-volume collection with over one hundred science fiction, fantasy, and horror stories from around the world, *Sunspot Jungle: The Ever Expanding Universe of Fantasy and Science Fiction.* Campbell lives in Washington, DC, where he spends his time with his family and helms Rosarium Publishing.

Bizhan Khodabandeh is a visual communicator who moves freely across the professional boundaries as designer, illustrator, artist, and activist. He has received numerous national and international awards for his work, including a silver medal from the Society of Illustrators (SI) for comics. His co-created books *Kitty Meow Meow*, written by his child, and *The Little Red Fish*, written by James Moffitt, have also been recognized by the SI. His work has been included anthologies such as: *New Frontiers: The Many Worlds of George Takei*, *APB*, *Sunspot Jungle*, and *Once Upon a Time Machine Vol 2*. Currently Khodabandeh teaches full-time at VCU's Robertson School of Media & Culture and freelances under the name Mended Arrow.

P. Djèlí Clark is the award-winning and Hugo, Nebula, Sturgeon, and World Fantasy nominated author of the novellas *Ring Shout, The Black God's Drums,* and *The Haunting of Tram Car 015*. His stories have appeared in online venues such as Tor.com, *Daily Science Fiction*, *Heroic Fantasy Quarterly*, *Apex*, *Lightspeed*, *Fireside*, *Beneath Ceaseless Skies*, and in print anthologies including *Griots*, *Hidden Youth*, and *Clockwork Cairo*. He is a founding member of *FIYAH* literary magazine and an infrequent reviewer at *Strange Horizons*.

About PM

PM Press is an independent, radical publisher of books and media to educate, entertain, and inspire. Founded in 2007 by a small group of people with decades of publishing, media, and organizing experience, PM Press amplifies the voices of radical authors, artists, and activists. Our aim is to deliver bold political ideas and vital stories to all walks of life and arm the dreamers to demand the impossible. We have sold millions of copies of our books, most often one at a time, face to face. We're old enough to know what we're doing and young enough to know what's at stake. Join us to create a better world.

PM Press
PO Box 23912
Oakland CA 94623
510-658-3906
www.pmpress.org

PM Press in Europe
europe@pmpress.org
www.pmpress.org.uk

Friends of PM

These are indisputably momentous times—the financial system is melting down globally and the Empire is stumbling. Now more than ever there is a vital need for radical ideas.

In the many years since its founding—and on a mere shoestring—PM Press has risen to the formidable challenge of publishing and distributing knowledge and entertainment for the struggles ahead. With hundreds of releases to date, we have published an impressive and stimulating array of literature, art, music, politics, and culture. Using every available medium, we've succeeded in connecting those hungry for ideas and information to those putting them into practice.

Friends of PM allows you to directly help impact, amplify, and revitalize the discourse and actions of radical writers, filmmakers, and artists. It provides us with a stable foundation from which we can build upon our early successes and provides a much-needed subsidy for the materials that can't necessarily pay their own way. You can help make that happen—and receive every new title automatically delivered to your door once a month—by joining as a Friend of PM Press. And, we'll throw in a free T-shirt when you sign up.

Here are your options:

- $30 a month: Get all books and pamphlets plus 50% discount on all webstore purchases
- $40 a month: Get all PM Press releases (including CDs and DVDs) plus 50% discount on all webstore purchases
- $100 a month: Superstar—Everything plus PM merchandise, free downloads, and 50% discount on all webstore purchases

For those who can't afford $30 or more a month, we have Sustainer Rates at $15, $10, and $5. Sustainers get a free PM Press T-shirt and a 50% discount on all purchases from our website.

Your Visa or Mastercard will be billed once a month, until you tell us to stop. Or until our efforts succeed in bringing the revolution around. Or the financial meltdown of Capital makes plastic redundant. Whichever comes first.

(H)afrocentric Comics:
Volumes 1-4

Juliana "Jewels" Smith
Illustrated by Ronald Nelson
Colors/Lettering by Mike Hampton
Foreword by Kiese Laymon

ISBN: 9781629634487
$20.00 • 136 pages

Glyph Award winner Juliana "Jewels" Smith and illustrator Ronald Nelson have created an unflinching visual and literary tour-de-force on the most pressing issues of the day—including gentrification, police violence, and the housing crisis—with humor and biting satire. *(H)afrocentric* tackles racism, patriarchy, and popular culture head-on. Unapologetic and unabashed, *(H)afrocentric* introduces us to strong yet vulnerable students of color, as well as an aesthetic that connects current Black pop culture to an organic reappropriation of hip hop fashion circa the early 90s.

We start the journey when gentrification strikes the neighborhood surrounding Ronald Reagan University. Naima Pepper recruits a group of disgruntled undergrads of color to combat the onslaught by creating and launching the first and only anti-gentrification social networking site, mydiaspora.com. The motley crew is poised to fight back against expensive avocado toast, muted Prius cars, exorbitant rent, and cultural appropriation.

Whether Naima and the gang are transforming social media, leading protests, fighting rent hikes, or working as "Racial Translators," the students at Ronald Reagan University take movements to a new level by combining their tech-savvy, Black Millennial sensibilities with their individual backgrounds, goals, and aspirations.

Crossroads: I Live Where I Like:
A Graphic History

Koni Benson
Illustrated by André Trantraal, Nathan Trantraal, and Ashley E. Marais
Foreword by Robin D.G. Kelley

ISBN: 978-1-62963-835-5
$20.00 • 168 pages

Drawn by South African political cartoonists the Trantraal brothers and Ashley Marais, *Crossroads: I Live Where I Like* is a graphic nonfiction history of women-led movements at the forefront of the struggle for land, housing, water, education, and safety in Cape Town over half a century. Drawing on over sixty life narratives, it tells the story of women who built and defended Crossroads, the only informal settlement that successfully resisted the apartheid bulldozers in Cape Town. The story follows women's organized resistance from the peak of apartheid in the 1970s to ongoing struggles for decent shelter today. Importantly, this account was workshopped with contemporary housing activists and women's collectives who chose the most urgent and ongoing themes they felt spoke to and clarified challenges against segregation, racism, violence, and patriarchy standing between the legacy of the colonial and apartheid past and a future of freedom still being fought for.

Presenting dramatic visual representations of many personalities and moments in the daily life of this township, the book presents a thoughtful and thorough chronology, using archival newspapers, posters, photography, pamphlets, and newsletters to further illustrate the significance of the struggles at Crossroads for the rest of the city and beyond. This collaboration has produced a beautiful, captivating, accessible, forgotten, and in many ways uncomfortable history of Cape Town that has yet to be acknowledged.

Crossroads: I Live Where I Like raises questions critical to the reproduction of segregation and to gender and generational dynamics of collective organizing, to ongoing anticolonial struggles and struggles for the commons, and to new approaches to social history and creative approaches to activist archives.

Maroon Comix:

Origins and Destinies

Edited by Quincy Saul
Illustrated by Seth Tobocman, Mac McGill, and Songe Riddle

ISBN: 9781629635712
$15.95 • 72 pages

Escaping slavery in the Americas, maroons made miracles in the mountains, summoned new societies in the swamps, and forged new freedoms in the forests. They didn't just escape ßand steal from plantations—they also planted and harvested polycultures. They not only fought slavery but proved its opposite, and for generations they defended it with blood and brilliance.

Maroon Comix is a fire on the mountain where maroon words and images meet to tell stories together. Stories of escape and homecoming, exile and belonging. Stories that converge on the summits of the human spirit, where the most dreadful degradation is overcome by the most daring dignity. Stories of the damned who consecrate their own salvation.

With selections and citations from the writings of Russell Maroon Shoatz, Herbert Aptheker, C.L.R. James, and many more, accompanied by comics and illustrations from Songe Riddle, Mac McGill, Seth Tobocman, Hannah Allen, Emmy Kepler, and Mikaela González. *Maroon Comix* is an invitation to never go back, to join hands and hearts across space and time with the maroons and the mountains that await their return.

Understanding Jim Crow:
Using Racist Memorabilia to Teach Tolerance and Promote Social Justice

David Pilgrim
Foreword by Henry Louis Gates Jr.

ISBN: 9781629631141
$24.95 • 208 pages

For many people, especially those who came of age after landmark civil rights legislation was passed, it is difficult to understand what it was like to be an African American living under Jim Crow segregation in the United States. Most young Americans have little or no knowledge about restrictive covenants, literacy tests, poll taxes, lynchings, and other oppressive features of the Jim Crow racial hierarchy. Even those who have some familiarity with the period may initially view racist segregation and injustices as mere relics of a distant, shameful past. A proper understanding of race relations in this country must include a solid knowledge of Jim Crow—how it emerged, what it was like, how it ended, and its impact on the culture.

Understanding Jim Crow introduces readers to the Jim Crow Museum of Racist Memorabilia, a collection of more than ten thousand contemptible collectibles that are used to engage visitors in intense and intelligent discussions about race, race relations, and racism. The items are offensive. They were meant to be offensive. The items in the Jim Crow Museum served to dehumanize blacks and legitimized patterns of prejudice, discrimination, and segregation.

Using racist objects as teaching tools seems counterintuitive—and, quite frankly, needlessly risky. Many Americans are already apprehensive discussing race relations, especially in settings where their ideas are challenged. The museum and this book exist to help overcome our collective trepidation and reluctance to talk about race.

Fully illustrated, and with context provided by the museum's founder and director David Pilgrim, *Understanding Jim Crow* is both a grisly tour through America's past and an auspicious starting point for racial understanding and healing.

Watermelons, Nooses, and Straight Razors:

Stories from the Jim Crow Museum

David Pilgrim
Foreword by Debby Irving

ISBN: 9781629634371
$24.95 • 272 pages

All groups tell stories, but some groups have the power to impose their stories on others, to label others, stigmatize others, paint others as undesirables—and to have these stories presented as scientific fact, God's will, or wholesome entertainment. *Watermelons, Nooses, and Straight Razors* examines the origins and significance of several longstanding antiblack stories and the caricatures and stereotypes that support them. Here readers will find representations of the lazy, childlike Sambo, the watermelon-obsessed pickaninny, the buffoonish minstrel, the subhuman savage, the loyal and contented mammy and Tom, and the menacing, razor-toting coon and brute.

Malcolm X and James Baldwin both refused to eat watermelon in front of white people. They were aware of the jokes and other stories about African Americans stealing watermelons, fighting over watermelons, even being transformed into watermelons. Did racial stories influence the actions of white fraternities and sororities who dressed in blackface and mocked black culture, or employees who hung nooses in their workplaces? What stories did the people who refer to Serena Williams and other dark-skinned athletes as apes or baboons hear? Is it possible that a white South Carolina police officer who shot a fleeing black man had never heard stories about scary black men with straight razors or other weapons? Antiblack stories still matter.

Watermelons, Nooses, and Straight Razors uses images from the Jim Crow Museum, the nation's largest publicly accessible collection of racist objects. These images are evidence of the social injustice that Martin Luther King Jr. referred to as "a boil that can never be cured so long as it is covered up but must be exposed to the light of human conscience and the air of national opinion before it can be cured." Each chapter concludes with a story from the author's journey, challenging the integrity of racial narratives.

The Real Cost of Prisons Comix

Edited by Lois Ahrens
Written by Ellen Miller-Mack, Craig Gilmore, Lois Ahrens, Susan Willmarth, and Kevin Pyle
Illustrated by Kevin Pyle, Sabrina Jones, and Susan Willmarth
Introduction by Craig Gilmore and Ruth Wilson Gilmore

ISBN: 9781604860344
$14.95 • 104 pages

Winner of the 2008 PASS Award (Prevention for a Safer Society) from the National Council on Crime and Delinquency

One out of every hundred adults in the U.S. One out of every hundred adults in the U.S. is in prison. This book provides a crash course in what drives mass incarceration, the human and community costs, and how to stop the numbers from going even higher. Collected in this volume are the three comic books published by the Real Cost of Prisons Project. The stories and statistical information in each comic book are thoroughly researched and documented.

Prison Town: Paying the Price tells the story of how the financing and site locations of prisons affects the people of rural communities in which prison are built. It also tells the story of how mass incarceration affects people of urban communities where the majority of incarcerated people come from.

Prisoners of the War on Drugs includes the history of the war on drugs, mandatory minimums, how racism creates harsher sentences for people of color, stories of how the war on drugs works against women, three strikes laws, obstacles to coming home after incarceration, and how mass incarceration destabilizes neighborhoods.

Prisoners of a Hard Life: Women and Their Children includes stories about women trapped by mandatory sentencing and the "costs" of incarceration for women and their families. Also included are alternatives to the present system, a glossary, and footnotes.

Over 125,000 copies of the comic books have been printed and more than 100,000 have been sent to people who are incarcerated, to their families, and to organizers and activists throughout the country. The book includes a chapter with descriptions of how the comix have been put to use in the work of organizers and activists in prison and in the "free world" by ESL teachers, high school teachers, college professors, students, and health care providers throughout the country. The demand for the comix is constant and the ways in which they are being used are inspiring.

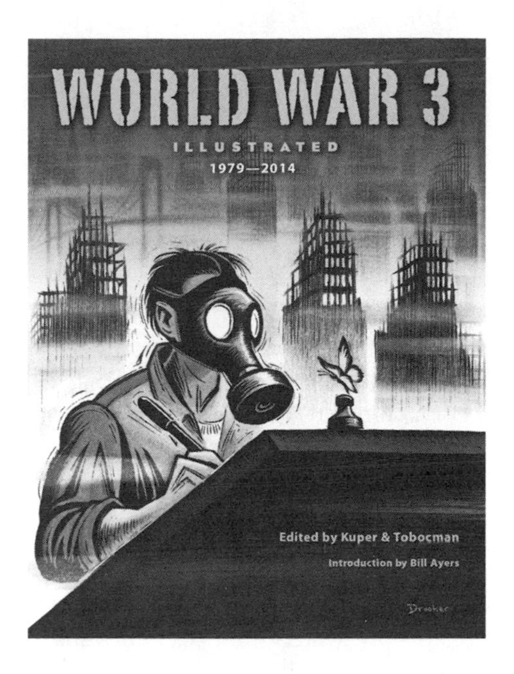

World War 3 Illustrated:
1979–2014

**Edited by Peter Kuper
and Seth Tobocman
Introduction by Bill Ayers**

ISBN: 9781604869583
$29.95 • 320 pages

Founded in 1979 by Seth Tobocman and Peter Kuper, *World War 3 Illustrated* is a labor of love run by a collective of artists (both first-timers and established professionals) and political activists working with the unified goal of creating a home for political comics, graphics, and stirring personal stories. Their confrontational comics shine a little reality on the fantasy world of the American kleptocracy, and have inspired the developing popularity and recognition of comics as a respected art form.

This full-color retrospective exhibition is arranged thematically, including housing rights, feminism, environmental issues, religion, police brutality, globalization, and depictions of conflicts from the Middle East to the Midwest. World War 3 Illustrated isn't about a war that may happen; it's about the ongoing wars being waged around the world and on our very own doorsteps. *World War 3 Illustrated* also illuminates the war we wage on each other—and sometimes the one taking place in our own minds. World War 3 artists have been covering the topics that matter for over 30 years, and they're just getting warmed up.

Contributors include Sue Coe, Eric Drooker, Fly, Sandy Jimenez, Sabrina Jones, Peter Kuper, Mac McGill, Kevin Pyle, Spain Rodriguez, Nicole Schulman, Seth Tobocman, Susan Willmarth, and dozens more.

The System

Peter Kuper
Introduction by Calvin Reid

ISBN: 9781604868111
$19.95 • 112 pages

Actions speak louder than words.

It's said that the flutter of insect wings in the Indian Ocean can send a hurricane crashing against the shores of the American Northeast. It's this premise that lies at the core of *The System*, a wordless graphic novel created and fully painted by award-winning illustrator Peter Kuper. From the subway system to the solar system, human lives are linked by an endless array of interconnecting threads. They tie each of us to our world and it to the universe. If every action has an equal and opposite reaction, get ready to run for cover!

A sleazy stockbroker is lining his pockets. A corrupt cop is shaking down drug dealers. A mercenary bomber is setting the timer. A serial killer is stalking strippers. A political scandal is about to explode. The planet is burning.
And nobody's talking.

Told without captions or dialogue, The System is an astonishing progression of vivid imagery, each brilliantly executed panel containing a wealth of information, with layer upon layer forming a vast and intricate tour of an ominous world of coincidences and consequences.

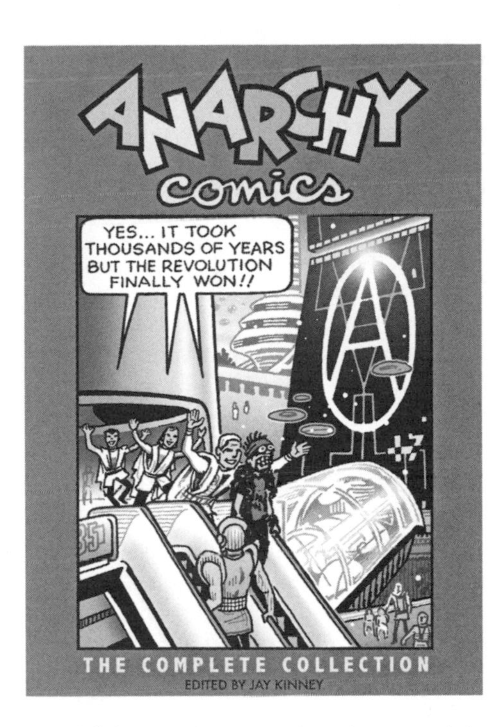

Anarchy Comics:
The Complete Collection

Jay Kinney

ISBN: 9781604865318
$20.00 • 224 pages

Anarchy Comics: The Complete Collection brings together the legendary four issues of *Anarchy Comics* (1978–1986), the underground comic that melded anarchist politics with a punk sensibility, producing a riveting mix of satire, revolt, and artistic experimentation. This international anthology collects the comic stories of all thirty contributors from the U.S., Great Britain, France, Germany, Netherlands, Spain, and Canada.

In addition to the complete issues of *Anarchy Comics,* the anthology features previously unpublished work by Jay Kinney and Sharon Rudahl, along with a detailed introduction by Kinney, which traces the history of the comic he founded and provides entertaining anecdotes about the process of herding an international crowd of anarchistic cats.

Contributors include: Jay Kinney, Yves Frémion, Gerhard Seyfried, Sharon Rudahl, Steve Stiles, Donald Rooum, Paul Mavrides, Adam Cornford, Spain Rodriguez, Melinda Gebbie, Gilbert Shelton, Volny, John Burnham, Cliff Harper, Ruby Ray, Peter Pontiac, Marcel Trublin, Albo Helm, Steve Lafler, Gary Panter, Greg Irons, Dave Lester, Marion Lydebrooke, Matt Feazell, Pepe Moreno, Norman Dog, Zorca, R. Diggs (Harry Driggs), Harry Robins, and Byron Werner.

Wildcat Anarchist Comics

Author and Illustrator: Donald Rooum
Foreword by Jay Kinney
Colorist: Jayne Clementson

ISBN: 9781629631271
$14.95 • 128 pages

Wildcat Anarchist Comics collects the drawings of Donald Rooum, mostly (but by no means entirely) from the long-running "Wildcat" cartoon series that has been published in Freedom newspaper since 1980. Rooum does not just purvey jokes but makes the drawings comical in themselves, "getting the humour in the line," provoking laughter even in those who do not read the captions or speech balloons.

The chief characters in the strip are the Revolting Pussycat, a short-fused anarchist who is furious and shouty; and the Free-Range Egghead, an intellectual who would like anarchism to be respectable but sometimes appears foolish. Governments, bosses, and authoritarians are presented as buffoons, and quite often so are anarchists. This thoughtful and delightful collection includes strips from The Skeptic and many more, all beautifully colored for the first time by Jayne Clementson.

The book also includes a lively autobiographical introduction that discusses Rooum's role in the 1963 "Challenor case," in which a corrupt police officer planted a weapon on Rooum at a demonstration, ultimately resulting in Rooum's acquittal.

Anarchy Comics: Slingshot: 40 Postcards by Eric Drooker

Author and Illustrator: Eric Drooker

ISBN: 9781629635088
$19.95 • 84 pages

Disguised as a book of innocent postcards, *Slingshot* is a dangerous collection of Eric Drooker's most notorious posters. Plastered on brick walls from New York to Berlin, tattooed on bodies from Kansas to Mexico City, Drooker's graphics continue to infiltrate and inflame the body politic. Drooker is the author of two graphic novels, *Flood! A Novel in Pictures* (winner of the American Book Award), and *Blood Song: A Silent Ballad*. He collaborated with Beat poet Allen Ginsberg on the underground classic *Illuminated Poems.* His provocative art has appeared on countless posters and book covers, and his hard-edged graphics are a familiar sight on street corners throughout the world. Eric Drooker is a third-generation New Yorker, born and raised on Manhattan Island. His paintings are frequently seen on covers of the New Yorker and hang in various art collections throughout the U.S. and Europe.

Revolutionary Women:
A Book of Stencils

Queen of the Neighbourhood

ISBN: 9781604862003
$14.00 • 128 pages

A radical feminist history and street art resource for inspired readers! This book combines short biographies with striking and usable stencil images of thirty women—activists, anarchists, feminists, freedom-fighters, and visionaries.

It offers a subversive portrait history which refuses to belittle the military prowess and revolutionary drive of women, whose violent resolves often shatter the archetype of woman-as-nurturer. It is also a celebration of some extremely brave women who have spent their lives fighting for what they believe in and rallying supporters in climates where a woman's authority is never taken as seriously as a man's. The text also shares some of each woman's ideologies, philosophies, struggles, and quiet humanity with quotes from their writings or speeches.

The women featured are: Harriet Tubman, Louise Michel, Vera Zasulich, Emma Goldman, Qiu Jin, Nora Connolly O'Brien, Lucia Sanchez Saornil, Angela Davis, Leila Khaled, Comandante Ramona, Phoolan Devi, Ani Pachen, Anna Mae Aquash, Hannie Schaft, Rosa Luxemburg, Brigitte Mohnhaupt, Lolita Lebron, Djamila Bouhired, Malalai Joya, Vandana Shiva, Olive Morris, Assata Shakur, Sylvia Rivera, Haydée Santamaría, Marie Equi, Mother Jones, Doria Shafik, Ondina Peteani, Whina Cooper, and Lucy Parsons.